Tend to Me

Tend to Me
Devotions for Mothers
Volume I

By Emily Cook

All Scripture quotations are from
The Holy Bible, English Standard Version® (ESV®),
Copyright © 2001 by Crossway, a publishing ministry
of Good News Publishers.
Used by permission. All rights reserved.

Cover Art by Michele Rockhill
http://jmrockhill.blogspot.com/

Copyright © 2012 Emily Cook
Permission granted to reproduce all or part of this
publication with due credit given to the author.

ISBN-13: 978-1480198883
ISBN-10: 1480198889

For those who tend to little people

Contents

Acknowledgments	
Introduction	1
Grasshoppers and Grace	5
Important Things	11
You're Doing it All Wrong	15
Adorable Blobs and God's Love	19
All Things to All People	25
Pushing Chairs Around the Room	29
Discontentment	33
Benched	37
Wounded Mommy	41
Grace and Casseroles	47
Judge Me and I'll Judge You Back	51
Missing the Obvious	55
Tangled	59
Bruises	63
Scowling	67
Kicking It In	73
Tending	77
What Do You Have that You Did Not Receive?	81
Held in Peace	85
Tired Explorer	89
Conclusion	93

Acknowledgments

I offer my heartfelt thanks to those dear people in my life who have encouraged, helped, and blessed me:

To Kathy Klumpp—my soul mate in motherhood, whose wisdom in the grammatical arts far exceeds mine. Thank you for your diligence, your patience, and your encouragement.

To Michele Rockhill—whose talent for things delicate, visual, and beautiful, amazes me. Thank you for sharing your creativity.

To my dear children—whose constant love reminds me of the grace of God, and whose constant presence drives me to hiding and writing. Thank you for giving me so much love, and writing material.

To my husband—whose hard work and for me and our children provides for our every need. Your strong faithfulness gives us the security to bloom, to grow, and to create. You are grace to me, and I thank God for you.

To my encouragers—those who are blessed by my words, and who let me know it from time to time. Thank you for encouraging me to use the gifts God has given me.

To God, who tends to me, faithfully, and gently, even as I tend to the little people in my home.

Introduction

I never realized how much I love peace and quiet until I had kids.

In my memory, there is version of myself that I miss. I am not thinking primarily of my skinny self, though I miss that, too. I recall a calm self, a self that had time to read books. I remember a self that could think on a subject logically, analyze, debate and discuss politics, religion, and literature. I remember a self that could go out in public without snot on her shoulder.

My young self dreamed of writing a book someday. It was to be a book like none other: on matters of life and death, destined to inspire millions, impress the academic world, and lead to the salvation of many souls.

I am no longer that person, and this is not that book.

When I go to the library nowadays, I do not bring an enormous backpack full of college textbooks. I bring a giant diaper bag. I do not look for a quiet corner for uninterrupted reading. My current library has no such quiet corner, especially when my six children and I are there. I still look for corners, but only for enforcing time-outs. I log into the computer, not to check email, but to start up phonics games, in hopes of entertaining a few kids while I chase after a few other kids. While puzzles are chewed and digital rabbits sing, I race around the library filling our bag with picture books.

Peace and quiet: when it permeated my days, I never appreciated it. Now it is so rare I hardly know what to do with it. From morning to night I am surrounded by six talkers, six bright-eyed, eager adventurers, six precious little sinners. My heart and my house are bursting with the sheer quantity of joy and work that fills this home. When the chatter dies down, the dishwasher runs, and the children are finally put in bed, what is a mother to do with herself?

She could collapse. I often do. She could spend time with her husband. I do not do that enough. She could play. She could have some sort of fun hobby, some sort of indulgent, stress-relieving, energizing diversion. She could eat something she likes, and not have to share or defend her choice to any little people. She could indulge her mind and body at the same time; eating while she ponders. I do all of these things.

My favorite hobby is playing with words. I leave the Rice Krispies on the floor while I type in my kitchen, and I amuse myself. I read, I write, I spend time with my nice, clean, cooperative word processor. I ponder the sweet and ugly moments in my day and re-create them with words. I take mental snapshots, wrap them in verbiage, sprinkle in some prayer, and frame them in cyberspace.

Words, all day long, spoken between children, spoken at me, spoken by me—words, like popcorn in the microwave, constant, loud, and unrelenting—I store them up by day, and digest them by night. The words that follow are words I offer to other mothers: words to entertain, encourage, and inspire you as you face a similar onslaught of unrelenting demands; words, I hope, that will bring you laughter and encouragement in your own rare moments of peace and quiet.

It is not the quantity of children, but it is the blessed weight of any number of children, that makes us what we are: mothers. We find that lost mitten, practice phonics in the car, and come up with creative ways to discipline; we hide in the shower, we collapse when the kids go to bed, we forget to take our vitamins even though we give them to the kids. We have bad days, when we raise our voices and we cringe when we hear the word "mommy." We have good days, when our hands willingly bake cookies and shape souls.

Our jobs are never done, and what did get done could have done better. Our hearts are too small, our bodies are too tired, to love these little people as they deserve to be loved.

The grace of God in Christ allows us to be honest about our vocation; to look to Him for what we lack, to take refuge under his grace when we feel the weight of our sin. Grace gives us the freedom to laugh at ourselves, and even lower our standards a little bit.

Sit with me, friend. Let us draw strength from each other and from God for this impossible, wonderful vocation of motherhood.

Jesus, Good Shepherd, tend to us.

Grasshoppers and Grace

Sometimes living with toddlers feels like walking through a field of grasshoppers. There are days when it is cute and fun, when I enjoy the thrill of running through a field and dancing in the wild. Then there are those other days: the days when all I really want to do is relax on a bug-free beach where everything is quiet, and orderly, and peaceful. But those grasshoppers keep on chirping, coming towards me demanding sippy cups, diaper changes, and bananas. I step towards the kitchen to get started and somehow send 20 more grasshoppers hopping away, whining and leaving messes as they go. They bounce off my arms, my head, they get in my face over and over as they chirp their demands at me. I take deep breaths, calmly trying to take another step, only to send out another swarm of messes and chirps.

What can you do in a field full of bugs? You can go into hiding, or you can yell and flail like a maniac.

Sometimes, I try to hide. This day, I turned on cartoons, and hid in the office to have a short pity party. It only took about two minutes for the grasshoppers to find me. My daughter came into the room and immediately started making messes. "Honey, don't touch that book," I said; and before my sentence was done she was explaining and arguing why she should touch the book, why she really, really wanted to touch the book. Already she is a skilled debater. If someone isn't listening, she just talks a little louder and a little faster, gets a little closer and never, NEVER takes a breath until she wins the battle.

Flailing and yelling ensued.

"I SAID, 'DON'T TOUCH THE BOOK!' LISTEN TO YOUR MOTHER! AAAAAHHHHHHH!"

She stopped touching the book. She looked up at me with those huge, brown eyes and tried hard to be strong, but her lower lip stuck out and began to quiver, and then she bawled. Her little heart was broken and bleeding, and I was the one who wounded her. And yet, she didn't run away from her angry Mama Bear. She ran into my arms. "Oh, Honey, I am so sorry," I said immediately; and as I hugged her back, I started to cry, too.

The world is out of balance when parents act like children. Why in the world am I entrusted with these precious little souls? That day I prayed, *Lord, protect my children from me. Protect them from the mix of selfishness and post-partum hormones that are wreaking havoc in my mind.* That look in my daughter's eyes — the I-thought-you-loved-me-Mommy look — is what comes to mind on Sundays when I stand with the church to confess "that I am by nature sinful and unclean." My sin, my selfishness, is poison, and it hurts even those who are most dear to me.

"Lord, have mercy" has been the prayer of the church for ages. What else can we say when we recognize our sin for what it is? And God's answer is so amazing, so unbelievable that we need reminding in a million ways. He *has* had mercy on us. We see His forgiving love in Jesus on the cross. He reminds us over and over in His Word and through His people.

That day, He reminded me through the love of my daughter. When I was at my worst, she blinked away her tears, threw her arms around my neck and covered me in sweet forgiveness.

Lord, forgive me when I fail my children, when I sin against them and You. Forgive my sin, cover it with the blood of Christ, and keep me safe under His cross. Amen.

For further reflection

But you, O Lord, are a God merciful and gracious; slow to anger and abounding in steadfast love and faithfulness. (Psalm 86:15)

1. When you run to God, confessing your sin, how does He respond?

2. Have you ever received a reminder of grace from your own child?

3. Read Romans 5:1-8:

> *Therefore, since we have been justified by faith, we have peace with God through our Lord Jesus Christ. Through him we have also obtained access by faith into this grace in which we stand, and we rejoice in hope of the glory of God. Not only that, but we rejoice in our sufferings, knowing*

that suffering produces endurance, and endurance produces character, and character produces hope, and hope does not put us to shame, because God's love has been poured into our hearts through the Holy Spirit who has been given to us. For while we were still weak, at the right time Christ died for the ungodly. For one will scarcely die for a righteous person—though perhaps for a good person one would dare even to die—but God shows his love for us in that while we were still sinners, Christ died for us.

What is the basis for our peace with God? What else do we receive with this gift?

4. Read Psalm 51. Consider your sins, and pray this psalm with David.

*Psalm 51
Have mercy on me, O God,
according to your steadfast love;
according to your abundant mercy
blot out my transgressions.
Wash me thoroughly from my iniquity,
and cleanse me from my sin!
For I know my transgressions,
and my sin is ever before me.
Against you, you only, have I sinned
and done what is evil in your sight,
so that you may be justified in your words
and blameless in your judgment.
Behold, I was brought forth in iniquity,
and in sin did my mother conceive me.
Behold, you delight in truth in the inward being,
and you teach me wisdom in the secret heart.
Purge me with hyssop, and I shall be clean;
wash me, and I shall be whiter than snow.*

Let me hear joy and gladness;
let the bones that you have broken rejoice.
Hide your face from my sins,
and blot out all my iniquities.
Create in me a clean heart, O God,
and renew a right spirit within me.
Cast me not away from your presence,
and take not your Holy Spirit from me.
Restore to me the joy of your salvation,
and uphold me with a willing spirit.
Then I will teach transgressors your ways,
and sinners will return to you.
Deliver me from bloodguiltiness, O God,
O God of my salvation,
and my tongue will sing aloud of your righteousness.
O Lord, open my lips,
and my mouth will declare your praise.
For you will not delight in sacrifice, or I would give it;
you will not be pleased with a burnt offering.
The sacrifices of God are a broken spirit;
a broken and contrite heart, O God, you will not despise.

Important Things

I don't have time for a sick kid! I grumble in my head, thinking of my too-long list of things I will be forced to ignore if he stays clingy like this all day long. *I have more important things to do than sit on the couch!*

Do you, really? The baby looks up at me. And I see him. I really *see* him.

He sits on my lap, fighting his sixth ear infection, and pleads with his eyes, "*Hold me, Mama.*" I sit a little longer. His tears stop, and he snuggles into my soft robe. He hiccups, then sighs a grateful sigh. He is content. For a moment, I am content, too.

He cannot pray, not with words. He is too young for that, I suppose. And yet if he had the words, what would he pray for? He probably would pray for pain relief. (We still have those drops in the cupboard.) He would pray for a cure for his illness. (Daddy is on his way with the antibiotics.) He would pray for love and comfort in the meantime. (Perhaps he would ask for a body like a soft pillow, warm, sympathetic arms.) And God would answer his prayer, by sending him his mother.

The words were not necessary. God provided before he asked. In this moment, I am that provision. Right now, today, I am the one who soothes him. I am a comforting embrace to this little child, *my* little child. I am God's hands of compassion to him, God's arms around Him in an afternoon nap. What could be more important?

Together, we sleep. It is good to be a child.

Father, comfort your children when they are sick, and use my arms and my hands to show them love. Amen

For further reflection

1. Is it hard for you to set aside your to-do list to comfort a sick or needy child? Why do you think this is?

2. What needs do your children have today?

3. What needs are *not* yours to meet? Pray about them now.

4. What needs might God want you to meet for your children today? Pray that God will equip you for those.

5. Complete this sentence: God uses my hands to provide for my children when I _____.

6. How is anyone capable of doing this enormous job? Read the verses below for help.

Now may the God of peace who brought again from the dead our Lord Jesus, the great shepherd of the sheep, by the blood of the eternal covenant, equip you with everything good that you may do his will, working in us that which is pleasing in his sight, through Jesus Christ, to whom be glory forever and ever. Amen. (Hebrews 13:20-22)

*All Scripture is breathed out by God and profitable for teaching, for reproof, for correction, and for training in righteousness, that the man of God may be complete, equipped for every good work.
(2 Timothy 3:16-17)*

You're Doing It All Wrong

"You're doing it all wrong!"

With my first child, that is exactly what I heard every time she cried. Surely, if I were a better mother, I could figure out the problem and fix it. But my little angel is crying! I must be doing something wrong!

Eventually I got over that. I learned that babies just cry. They cry to express their needs. They cry because they want to be changed or they *don't* want to be changed. They cry because they hate getting dressed, or because they can't tell you why they're crying. But none of these reasons means I am doing something wrong.

Now, in this wild house of six young children, there are many other things that shout this accusation at me daily:

The children are fighting, again. I must be doing it wrong.

I am frustrated to the point of tears. I must be doing it wrong.

Someone STILL has a rebellious attitude. I must be doing it wrong.

I am feeling overwhelmed. I must be doing it wrong.

At the end of the day, I am WORN OUT. I must be doing it wrong.

Trouble comes into my vocation, strife without and within, and I cry out, "NO! This is not how life should be! I must be doing something wrong!" Tell me, isn't there a way to eliminate all this conflict, stress, and plain old hard work from the vocation of motherhood?

Maybe someone should ask that family how they do it. You know, THAT family, the one with the kids who never fight and the mother who never yells and at the end of the day they hug goodnight cheerfully and mother sits down to mend socks while she discusses current events with her husband.

I don't actually know that family. I just know that we certainly are *not* that family.

Surely, empowered by Christ, we ought to have that perfect life here and now, right? Shouldn't we be able to handle all things with calm, loving, selfless objectivity? Shouldn't we be immune to the effects of sin in ourselves and other people? So, if my life is not perfect, if I find it has trouble, I need to work really hard to figure out exactly what it is I am doing wrong, so that I can fix it! Right?

It's difficult to let go of the illusion of the perfect life. And I will not let it go as long as I think the imperfections are caused by something I actually can fix. I will chase after that dream. I will look under every rock for that magical solution that will rid my life of trouble and stress forever. I *will* find that magic potion that will make little boys BEHAVE!

But the imperfect life is not a problem I can fix. Sin is at its root: mine, theirs, and the side-effects of it in this fallen world. We still must live in this place, for a little while longer.

So I have this vocation, just like you, and in it I can expect trouble: trouble when I *am* doing it wrong, and trouble when I'm not. But, it will only be this way for a little while longer. God has promised to finish the work He has started. So, even as I whine along with the kids, I can take comfort in His unfailing grace.

Soon, very soon, the babies and the big people will be comforted together.

And the mommas will lie down with the little boys, and there will be peace.

Father, Help me to change what I can change, and to turn to you for strength to endure the things I cannot.

For further reflection

1. If you did every one of your jobs perfectly today, do you think your child would be happy all day long?

2. Does your child's unhappiness ever make you think you are doing something wrong? In what ways?

3. Sometimes, Mother, you do things wrong. You sin. What then?

If we say we have no sin, we deceive ourselves, and the truth is not in us. If we confess our sins, he is faithful and just to forgive us our sins and to cleanse us from all unrighteousness. (1 John 1:8-9)

4. Do you think it is a good idea to admit your sin to your child? Why or why not?

5. Do your children ever sin against you? How do you respond?

6. If we are walking with Jesus, do you think we can expect less conflict in our lives?

7. What comfort do we have in Jesus in the midst of our exhausting vocation?

> *For by grace you have been saved through faith. And this is not your own doing; it is the gift of God, not a result of works, so that no one may boast. (Ephesians 2:8-9)*

Adorable Blobs and God's Love

As I write this, we are anticipating the birth and baptism of yet another child. I have been here before; but each and every time I am more amazed at the miracle of life. There is just something about newborns that makes all of us a little crazy. Even grown men will make faces and say gushy things like "sweet pea," and "love muffin" to their children or grandchildren. The affection people pile on these new babies is unbelievable.

And what do the babies do with all this attention? When they hear, "Oh, what a precious little nose!" do they grimace and say, "Actually, I think it is a little too big." When they hear, "Oh, wow, he rolled over! He's going to be a genius!" do they explain that they are doing no more than every other baby before them has done, that they really are not nearly as special as their loved ones think they are? But a crazy statement like, "That was such a good burp, Honey!" is enough to draw a smile of pride on a baby's face. They eat up this attention. They delight in being loved, not for anything they have done, but for simply existing.

It is wonderful to be around passive little babies that we love just for being present. They eat, they sleep, they lay around all day — puking, messing, adorable little blobs. They observe, they learn, and they soak up our love.

It is amazing how the Lord pours out His love on our littlest ones. He asks nothing from them. He does not call them to the baptismal font because He knows in the future they will be great saints for His kingdom. He does not require bold statements of commitment on their part. He does not require that they prove themselves first. They are completely passive. They cannot even bring themselves to the font. Yet the Lord has made a way. He has placed in the hearts of parents a tiny taste of that gracious love. Parents so love their children that they eagerly bring them to Him. And He welcomes them with open arms.

Yet, when we adults get a taste of that kind of love for ourselves, what do we do? We come to church and are told, "It's good to see you," We hear again the sweet words, "Your sins are forgiven!" Does a smile ever cross your lips at that moment, as you are loved simply for being there? We are told, "Take, eat, this is my body!" When we come to the table, do we take a moment to bask in His love like newborns?

Adult believers would do well to remember this love of our Lord. Even we who were baptized as adorable blobs sometimes forget the unbelievable, undeserved affection by which we were made part of God's family. The next time you see one of God's newest little lambs, rejoice in the radical love of Jesus. Rejoice that He welcomes the littlest ones with open arms. And always remember that this is the same grace that welcomes you.

Father,
Thank you for giving me life and eternal life in Christ, not for anything I have done, but simply out of fatherly goodness and love. In Jesus, Amen

For further reflection

O Lord, you have searched me and known me!
You know when I sit down and when I rise up;
    you discern my thoughts from afar.
You search out my path and my lying down
    and are acquainted with all my ways.
Even before a word is on my tongue,
    behold, O Lord, you know it altogether.
You hem me in, behind and before,
    and lay your hand upon me.
Such knowledge is too wonderful for me;
    it is high; I cannot attain it.
Where shall I go from your Spirit?
    Or where shall I flee from your presence?
If I ascend to heaven, you are there!
    If I make my bed in Sheol, you are there!
If I take the wings of the morning
    and dwell in the uttermost parts of the sea,
even there your hand shall lead me,
    and your right hand shall hold me.
If I say, "Surely the darkness shall cover me,
    and the light about me be night,"
even the darkness is not dark to you;

> *the night is bright as the day,*
> *for darkness is as light with you.*
> *For you formed my inward parts;*
> *you knitted me together in my mother's womb.*
> *I praise you, for I am fearfully and wonderfully made.*
> *Wonderful are your works;*
> *my soul knows it very well.*
> *My frame was not hidden from you,*
> *when I was being made in secret,*
> *intricately woven in the depths of the earth.*
> *Your eyes saw my unformed substance;*
> *in your book were written, every one of them,*
> *the days that were formed for me,*
> *when as yet there was none of them.*
> *(Psalm 139:1-16)*

1. What do you learn from this Psalm about the way God regards your baby?

2. Do you say ridiculous things to your babies as you love them for simply existing?

3. Do you ever think God could feel that way about YOU? Read Psalm 139 again, and this time, remember that it applies to you, too.

4. Read Luke 18:15-17:

> *Now they were bringing even infants to him that he might touch them. And when the disciples saw it, they rebuked them. But Jesus called them to him, saying, "Let the children come to me, and do not hinder them, for to such belongs the kingdom of God. Truly, I say to you, whoever does not receive the kingdom of God like a child shall not enter it."*

Picture yourself as the one bringing the child to Jesus. Can you bring your child to Jesus like this today?

5. Would you love your child less if he were sick? Rebellious?

6. Read Luke 18:15-17 again. Picture yourself as the child welcomed by Jesus.

All Things to All People

He still is not sleeping AND he woke his sister? The audacity of that kid! The naughtiness, the selfish ingratitude of this child! A child who never has wanted for a thing in his life, taking a vacation from his normal easy pre-school life for even easier, more exciting days of vacation and family, not asked even once to wash a dish or change a diaper, sitting in his bed with a smirk on his face, refusing to grant me the one request I have made of him today: to take a nap!

A transgression and a smirking sinner led to a mommy fit; and a child crumbling under law spewing from my mouth in anger. Law he deserved, to be sure; but rage, he did not. I paused, prayed, breathed deeply. He cried.

"Just sit quietly while I figure out what I am going to do with you." I wanted to storm out of the camper and tell his father to deal with him.

I sat on the bench, arms crossed, and I tried to pray. *Jesus, help. What do I do with this kid? He has crumbled, and he was in the wrong. And, yes, I know I was, too; but I am just so frustrated!*

My son lay on his bed, staring at me while I pray, pleading with his eyes for reconciliation between us.

Finally, I sat beside him, still angry but also humbled, and spoke to him of sin. "Naughtiness, sin, hurts us and those around us, doesn't it?" He agreed, and, though he was young, he could understand see how his sin hurt, and he felt the sting of mine. We spoke of the wages of sin, of the cross, and of grace. We prayed and confessed together, and I reminded both of us of the forgiveness we have in Jesus.

We hugged afterward, but I could see in his eyes that he still was worried. He apologized one more time, and hugged me tightly, and one more time I told him that forgiven sin is not to bother us any longer. Yet, it seemed like such an abstract concept for this little guy. His regret still streamed from his eyes, and he continued to grovel.

"Sin IS very bad, son," I explained. "Like..." *hm, something little boys care about,* "like yucky poop. Have you ever seen a big pile of yucky poop on your toilet paper?"

Suddenly, his eyes were dancing. He nodded, knowing exactly what I was talking about. His nose wrinkled and he giggled.

"Yes, it's gross, isn't it? Well, sin is like having a big wad of gross toilet paper in your hands. But when we give it to God, do you know what he does with it? He forgives us. He flushes it down the toilet. Now, do you have to worry about your nasty toilet paper once it has been flushed away?"

"No," he shook his head and laughed.

"It's the same thing with sin. Once God forgives our sin, he flushes it away, and we don't have to worry about it. Isn't that great?"

His smile was huge and relieved. His mood was transformed. He hugged me one last time, and then settled down for his nap. We were at peace with each other and at peace with God.

I was left wondering about this conversation. Is this a good way for a mother of little boys to be "all things to all people," like Paul? And, will this child, for the rest of his life, ponder the grace of God every time he flushes the toilet?

Father, give me the patience and love I need for this day. When I fail, point me to Your love for me on the cross. Teach me to point the children to You, too, in words they understand. Amen

For further reflection

1. What do you think about comparing sin to yucky poop?

2. Read 1 Corinthians 9:19-23:

For though I am free from all, I have made myself a servant to all, that I might win more of them. To the Jews I became as a Jew, in order to win Jews. To those under the law I became as one under the law (though not being myself under the law) that I might win those under the law. To those outside the law I became as one outside the law (not being outside the law of God but under the law of Christ) that I might win those outside the law. To the weak I became weak, that I might win the weak. I have become all things to all people, that by all means I might save some. I do it all for the sake of the gospel, that I may share with them in its blessings.

WHY does Paul try to be "all things to all people?"

3. Do you ever lose your temper with your child? What types of situations tend to push you over the edge and into sin?

4. Have you ever confessed your sins TO your child? How did your child respond?

5. Read James 5:16:

> *Therefore, confess your sins to one another and pray for one another, that you may be healed.*

What do you think a child learns when his mother confesses a sin?

6. Read 1 John 1:9:

> *If we confess our sins, he is faithful and just to forgive us our sins and to cleanse us from all unrighteousness.*

What are we supposed to do when we sin? What does God do in response?

Pushing Chairs Around the Room

"What are you trying to do? Can I help you?"

I asked this question in response to the screams I heard from the other room. First, I heard the sound of moving furniture, then a small crash, followed by screams. They were screams of frustration, so I did not run, but finished what I was doing, took some deep breaths, and then walked into the room to see what the problem was.

My little son had gotten in his mind that he wanted to move the chairs around the dining room. However, he is not quite old enough to be able to plan ahead very far, nor can he articulate exactly what it is he is trying to do. He simply toddled up to a chair, grabbed it with his fat little hands, and used every bit of his tiny body to make it move. It got stuck on a table leg. Without wasting time trying to problem-solve, he immediately switched into scream-and-cry mode.

So I asked, "Can I help you, Honey?"

"AARRRGGGHHH!!!" The screams became higher pitched, and he threw himself on the floor. In my motherly wisdom, I saw that my old standby tactic ("Do I need to separate you two?") would not work this time. Perhaps separation from that particular chair would help; but who can separate a child from all uncooperative, inanimate objects?

"Honey, where are you trying to take that?" He got up, hit the chair, screamed, and fell back on the floor. I tried to re-direct him. I quickly scooped him up, and I sat with him on the couch.

"Let's read a book," I suggested. He climbed off my lap, ran back to the chair, and smacked it again. Again, he screamed. I was getting a bit frustrated, too. "Honey, what is the big deal? Nobody even asked you to do that!" In frustration I took him out of the room, and when the screaming still did not stop, I sat him in the corner until he calmed down.

Nobody even asked you to do that. The words came out of my mouth, and again, I saw myself in this irrational child. How many times in my day do I get frustrated because I am unable to accomplish things that nobody even asked me to do?

It takes a good deal of wisdom to prioritize all the things on a list. I have not this wisdom, and so I am often frustrated. I recall the craft that seemed like a great idea; the laundry I wanted to get done today (not tomorrow); the potty-training session none of us were ready for; the little things that never get finished. Surely, if I got all of these things done, then I would have time and patience to deal with all of these childish interruptions!

Though I confine my own fit-throwing to the inside of my head (on my better days), I had to admit that I do understand my son's frustration over things that seem like nothing to anyone else who might be watching.

God, keep me from the folly of pushing chairs aimlessly around the room today. Help me to recognize what is important! Amen.

For further reflection

1. Do you have a hard time figuring out which things are most important for you to get done each day?

2. When you are uncertain about what to do, do you go to God's Word first? Do you immediately stop to pray? Why is this so hard for us to do?

3. Do you ever find yourself frustrated because you cannot finish something that nobody even asked you to do? Name something.

4. When your child interrupts you before you finish something, how do you handle it?

5. Read John 6:29:

> *Jesus answered them, "This is the work of God, that you believe in him whom he has sent."*

What does this tell us about our most important task each day?

6. Read Psalm 119:5:

> *Oh that my ways may be steadfast in keeping your statutes!*

Do you use God's Word to direct your path? In what ways? Write down a specific Scripture that has given you guidance.

7. Read Luke 10:27:

> *"You shall love the Lord your God with all your heart and with all your soul and with all your strength and with all your mind, and your neighbor as yourself."*

We are called to love God and to love our neighbor. This is our first and most important task each day. Mother, remember, next to your husband, *your children* are your nearest neighbors. How might this change the way you view the constant interruptions?

Discontentment

As the children squawk, "I want to sit by you for the movie, Mama!" wrestling and pushing and climbing over each other to get to me, I try to pry them apart and make room for everyone.

"Easy, kiddos. There's enough of Mommy to go around," I say. I say it quite often, yet they never seem to believe me.

They struggle with each other, always needing, always asking Mommy for whatever it is they need. I give what I can, though sometimes they must wait, and sometimes they must hear the word "no." Nobody is really starving, nobody is naked, and nobody has been left at the grocery store. Isn't that proof, dear children, that there really is enough of Mommy to go around?

But, honestly, there's not.

Were it possible, strictly by my own effort, to make my children become and stay content, I think it would have happened by now. But most often, at the end of the day, my efforts are spent, and still they are not content. I say this not to play the martyr. I say it because, again, I see myself in them.

I also am not content. I am restless, I am disappointed, or I am frustrated every single day. There is usually someone or something to blame for this. The children are uncooperative. My husband is too busy. My house is messy. My head hurts. My dog ran away, again. If these things were not so, would I be content then? Would I, if my husband spent 100% of his day doing my bidding and telling me how wonderful I am? Would I be content if my children were kind and clean and healthy, and my body never hurt, and the stupid dog stayed where I put him? The truth is, even if today was the first day that every single thing in my life went according to plan, tomorrow would not be that way, and the bit of contentment I felt today would disappear.

My children see me as the "Ultimate Need Meeter" in their lives, but when I daily fail to meet every one of their needs, they are disappointed. Their desire for their mother to meet all of their needs will surely change as they grow, and already is changing. Yet restless striving for contentment will not go away. They will try to satisfy themselves in their friends, in their studies, or in their young loves. Someday they will try to find contentment in their spouses, or their careers, or even their own children. I like that they need me, but my children need more than just me. And I need more than just them. What is it we need to be truly content? We want our needs met now, and we want to know that whatever needs we have in the future will also be met. We are restless because, even if our health and our relationships are intact today, we have no assurance that things will go well for us tomorrow. Those we love are unpredictable. Sometimes they sin and fail us, sometimes they get sick and fail us, sometimes they are called by God to serve people other than us. Sometimes God calls them to Himself, and away from us. This is simply the reality of life in this fallen world.

But God does not fail us. Only He can give us our daily bread today, and only He can promise to do it for us again tomorrow. The gifts He gives may not be those gifts we think we need so badly. It may not be all the motherly attention the children want, it may not be the clean house I want, but He abundantly gives to His children those things that truly are best. He gives forgiveness and destroys sin. He gives and sustains life. He gives breath to us who are but dust. He gives us Jesus.

Heavenly Father, teach us to desire the good things that You have to give us. The troubles in this fallen world and the confusion of our own hearts create discontentment for us daily. Help us to look to You for comfort and security during our journey here. Mercifully provide daily bread to both body and soul, and sustain us in Jesus until that glorious day when Your Kingdom finally comes. In the name of Jesus, the Bread of Life, Amen.

For further reflection

1. Mother, is it possible for you alone to meet all of your child's needs? Is this hard for you to accept?

2. "I just want my child to be happy." Many state this as their number one goal as parents. We all want our children to be happy. Yet, is it possible for them to be perfectly happy in this world?

3. What things, other than God, make you feel content, at least for a short period of time?

4. As we strive for personal contentment, what sorts of things get in our way?

5. "They will try to satisfy themselves with their friends, in their studies, with their young loves. They will someday try to find contentment in their spouses, or their careers, or even their own children." Do you try to find contentment in any of these things? Does it work?

6. Read 2 Corinthians 12: 7-10:

> *So to keep me from becoming conceited because of the surpassing greatness of the revelations, a thorn was given me in the flesh, a messenger of Satan to harass me, to keep me from becoming conceited. Three times I pleaded with the Lord about this, that it should leave me. But he said to me, "My grace is sufficient for you, for my power is made perfect in weakness." Therefore I will boast all the more gladly of my weaknesses, so that the power of Christ may rest upon me. For the sake of Christ, then, I am content with weaknesses, insults, hardships, persecutions, and calamities. For when I am weak, then I am strong.*

What drove Paul to pray? Should we pray about the things that cause us discontentment?

7. What was God's answer to Paul's prayer?

8. What is the reason for Paul's contentment?

9. How does this apply to your life as a mother?

Benched

I don't like being benched. As wearisome as it is to do what I have to do, day after day, in this house of six kids, it wearies me much more *not* to do it, to watch others do it for me. One week, due to a nasty cold, I had to sit for two days "on the bench" while the game went on without me.

Here are a few of my observations from the bench.

God does provide. Not even my children have wanted for anything. That's quite a thing to say considering their many needs, but God provided abundant help.

It is difficult to accept charity. It is difficult to receive kindness that I never can repay. May God uphold and bless those who are so kind as to share my burden.

I don't consider it all charity. I noticed something in my heart this time that surprised me: *I don't count my husband as charity.* In fact, I think he owes it to me. Isn't this what a helpmate is for? They are his kids too, right? I am quite eager to put part of my burden on his shoulders, whereas I tend to try to be tougher when it comes to offers of help from others.

This is a hard one to sort out, indeed. Of course it is good to rely most heavily on the flesh of my flesh, and helpmates are for helping. But where is this sense of entitlement coming from? Have I been unconsciously "keeping score" of the things we do around the house, and now seems to be a good time to cash in? Again, sin! Sin in my love towards my husband, making it plain that his help is gracious indeed!

It is good to slow down and listen. My recent malady involved much fatigue, so that I couldn't sit at my computer and type, and I couldn't even hold my Ipod to surf the web while I lay in bed. Oh, the headlines that went unread! Sad and pathetic was I! Because it was all I could do, I listened. I closed my eyes and listened. I did not check my email, I did not look up something, I did not even clean something while I listened. I *just* listened. Wow, how listening feeds my soul!

My kids know how to care for me. No, they did not turn into perfect angels. Many a fight went unresolved among the boys while I was sick. Yet, I had opportunity to receive compassion from my children. I overheard whispered conspiracies of "trying to be really-super-good today." Not only did I receive get well cards, but routine chores were done without reminders, and the older children looked for extra ways to help. "Mommy, I cleaned this for you!" Wow, that sentence really does make me feel better! Another child with a great love for ice water filled my glass for me, waited until it was nice and cold, then reminded me to drink throughout the day. I really, truly needed this reminder. How amazing to experience God's care for me from my very own little children.

And how good it is to have the energy to change diapers and make jokes with the children again today.

Thank You, God, for carrying me through sickness, for providing for my children when I cannot. Thank you also for returned strength, and for this moment of health. Amen.

For further reflection

1. Do you have a hard time accepting help from others? Why do you think this is?

2. Read Galatians 6:2:

Bear one another's burdens, and so fulfill the law of Christ.

Is it OK to accept help? Is it OK to ask for it?

3. Do you find yourself more likely to accept help from some people than others? Why do you think this is so?

4. Do you ever catch yourself "keeping score" with those closest to you?

5. How does God provide for your family when you are sick?

Wounded Mommy

Some days are defined by that THING, that one very loud thought, that worry, prayer, or problem that refuses to leave me alone. At one time it was epilepsy, but it has been everything from church problems to health problems to someone else's problems to something in the news. It is a heaviness on the heart, with a strong gravitational pull. I may be able to wrest my thoughts free for a moment; but the second I am not preoccupied, the concern sucks my thoughts right back to itself and tries to consume me. I know I must begin days like this with prayer. Even when I do this, what often follows is a day of futile coping and very little relief. I do not have an easy answer for this kind of day, but I would like to put words to some of the things I know do NOT work, and share some of my favorite crutches.

That kind of day
The heavy thing is there on my heart, invading my thoughts even before my feet hit the floor. I linger in bed to pray about it; but long before I am ready, little feet stomp down the hallway, and little bodies crawl into my bed demanding cartoons and food. I sigh. How do I enter the world of childhood joy and noise and frivolous "crises," one after another, when this cloud hangs so heavily?

Chasing the wind—futile coping measures I have tried repeatedly

Solitude: Perhaps I ought to hide from the kids so I can obsess over my concern. It is taking up so much of my attention that I know I am going to be short with them anyway. I might as well hide.

Mental gymnastics: If I work on it for a little while, maybe I can contort my mind in just the right way so that the concern will go away.

Numbing: Perhaps I can try really hard to kill the feelings associated with my concern. THEN I can return to my vocation.

Demanding the above through prayer: God, here's my problem. Can you make the kids leave me alone today so we can talk about it until my concern is resolved? Or, you could take it utterly out of my mind please, and let me get back to life?

There is a false presupposition underneath all of this "coping": *I cannot do my job with this heavy thing on my heart.*

What do you mean by this, self?

I do not want to do my job with this heavy thing on my heart. I know I cannot do it well. I cannot do it perfectly. I cannot do it even as well as I normally do it. I am tired and emotional. *Lord, can't I just take a personal day?*

On normal days, I am much more capable of being a patient, fun mommy. If I didn't have all these distractions, I could be that mommy who skips cheerfully with her well-groomed, cooperative little flock, singing hymns as we frolic joyfully down the path of righteousness. Well, maybe not. So, today I will not do my job perfectly. Today will be imperfect, just like yesterday.

It is true, I cannot do my job *perfectly* when I am carrying a heavy heart, when I am limping with some kind of wound. And in my experience, God doesn't just make those kinds of things vanish when we ask Him to. Sometimes even in the midst of our vocation, we must limp. Sometimes, instead of instant healing, He offers crutches.

I cannot be normal Mommy on days when I am *not* normal Mommy, when my heart is weighed down by one of the million griefs of this life. Yet I can still be Mommy. Wounded Mommy *can* still be Mommy.

However, mommies are not machines. We cannot perform the same tasks in the same way day after day after day. We are affected by events, weather, hormones, health, and problems of all kinds. Some seasons we move about on healthy legs with no limping, but in others, we mother with injuries; and when we are injured, we would be crazy not to use crutches.

So, children, wounded Mommy is going to do things a little bit differently than normal Mommy. She is going to lower her standards, and she WILL be using crutches.

My favorite crutches

Work it out. Good, sweaty exercise can be cleansing and invigorating.

Shorten the list. Eliminate anything that requires extra energy or extra patience that is not absolutely necessary. Wounded Mommy cannot do crafts; she cannot let you paint; she will not let children "help" make cookies; and she probably will not be up for a wrestling match. This is OK.

Enforce quiet time. In the afternoon, the children will nap or read in another room. They shall not come out of their rooms until mom says so, period.

Receive God's gifts through His Word and hymns. Wounded Mommy must do this frequently throughout the day, even if she has to lock herself in the bathroom for a minute or two.

Get outside. Soak up the sounds, sights, and smells of God's creation.

Receive help offered. Just accept it as grace, like the air you breathe.

Ask for help. Don't hint, just ask. (I am still learning this one.)

See the doctor. It is good to seek God's help from your doctor for medical problems.

Explain yourself. If they are old enough, tell your children why you are "limping" today. Their compassion may surprise you.

Eat. Food is comforting, and God intends it to be so. I often receive grace through mashed potatoes.

Look at the children. Really *look* at those God has given you to love. Take a real time-out, refusing to work on whatever else it is you think you need to do, banishing worry for a few minutes if possible. Get down on the floor, and *look* at those blessed details that make children unique, listen to their laughter, and do something with them that is fun for mom, too.

Pray. Pray constantly.

Lord, help me to care for these children despite my own aching heart. Teach me to love even when I am hurting. Help me to remember that it is not the children's fault that this world is fallen; nor is it my husband's, nor the dog's. Keep the pain from turning into anger and hurting those I love. Equip me for those acts of love You require me to do today, and show me what I can let go so that I can rest in You and heal. Thank you for your tender care for me when I am limping. In the name of Jesus, Amen.

For further reflection

1. How do you cope with heavy-hearted days? Have you tried any of the author's futile coping measures?

2. Read Isaiah 40:11:

> He will tend his flock like a shepherd;
> he will gather the lambs in his arms;
> he will carry them in his bosom,
> and gently lead those that are with young.

When has God demonstrated His gentle care for you?

3. What kinds of crutches does God send you?

4. Do you think it is OK to lower standards and take time for healing and rest? Is it hard for you to do this?

5. Read Matthew 11:25-30:

Jesus declared, "I thank you, Father, Lord of heaven and earth, that you have hidden these things from the wise and understanding and revealed them to little children; yes, Father, for such was your gracious will. All things have been handed over to me by my Father, and no one knows the Son except the Father, and no one knows the Father except the Son and anyone to whom the Son chooses to reveal him. Come to me, all who labor and are heavy laden, and I will give you rest. Take my yoke upon you, and learn from me, for I am gentle and lowly in heart, and you will find rest for your souls. For my yoke is easy, and my burden is light."

What do you learn about the heart of Jesus?

What does He invite you to do?

6. Do you have a collection of hymns or favorite verses for use on these difficult days? If not, consider making one this week.

Grace and Casseroles

Sometimes I wonder whether I actually listen to what I am saying. I stand there in the presence of God, with you, every Sunday, and I confess that I am "by nature sinful and unclean," and I pray "Lord, have mercy." I stand there with only my sins to offer, and I can do nothing but receive His grace. I beg. He gives. Ho hum.

Then I leave church with my children in tow, including one very naughty little boy, and somebody offers to help us home. "No thanks," I smile, "we're doing just fine." It seems like the right thing to say, even though I am practically limping from the bruise on my leg that he just gave me. He frees his hand from mine, and runs away. I wonder whether people can hear my blood boiling; but I keep walking, and I keep smiling.

I do not want to be a charity case. I have my life under control, for the most part—really I do. Yes, I need God, just as you do; but let's not take it too far, now. I'll open my hands to receive the free gift of salvation, but a ride home? A casserole? That's just too much!

Why do I think like this? Why do I squirm when help is offered? Why do I refuse to ask when help is needed?

I remember when seizures invaded, and everything was sickness and worry and the threat of death. I remember when I was empty, and everyone was needy, and I could not help because I was needy, too. I had no choice but to accept help: help from God, and help from people. I racked up debt after debt of kindness that I never can repay.

Then, I understood it clearly: I *am* a charity case. I am needy. I am weak. I am at His mercy.

But He *always* has mercy on me. He strengthens me through His Word and Sacraments, and sometimes (grace upon grace!) He helps me in very practical ways through His flesh-and-blood children.

Jesus is God in the flesh, and He shed his blood for me, for my salvation. Every other gift I receive is another drop of His love from this fountain. It is not necessary to keep track of the casserole debts. It is only necessary to be His child. As His child, I am learning to keep my hands open, to look for and receive His gifts of all kinds.

And sometimes, I get to be the one who gives the casserole.

Heavenly Father,
You have promised never to leave us or forsake us. Thank you, God, for keeping that promise to us. Thank you for Your life-giving Word and Sacraments. Thank you for the Church, Your Body, that is Your hand to embrace those who are suffering. When we are in need, help us to make our needs known to each other. Keep us from proud self-reliance, from living with closed hands and refusing to receive your practical gifts. Thank you for being a God who pours out love on all of us charity cases. Fill us to overflowing, that we may, in turn, share grace upon grace with our fellow Christians in need. In Jesus' name, Amen.

For further reflection

1. Do you ever pretend you are "fine" when you are not? Why do you think we do this?

2. Do you find it easier to receive the forgiveness of God in Christ than practical help from other people?

3. Have you ever received a gift with "strings attached," an obligation that you were expected to repay? How is this kind of giving different from the way God gives?

4. Read Romans 6:23:

> *For the wages of sin is death, but the free gift of God is eternal life in Christ Jesus our Lord.*

Do you receive charity from God, or does He make you earn it? Does this make you a charity case, at least before God?

5. "Every other gift I receive is another drop of His love from this fountain." Is this true? How does this change your perspective?

Judge Me and I'll Judge You Back

I always feel awkward around well-dressed people. If I know I am going to be interacting with such people, and I have time to prepare, I actually will try to put on makeup and change out of my cracker-covered clothes into something a little more presentable.

I had a doctor's appointment one day (no kids allowed: an outing, a break!) I actually took out the ponytail and wore my hair down, a feat typically reserved for (some) Sundays. Frumpy clothes are great for scrubbing floors, but today I get to leave the house! I need to look like I belong in the outside world!

As I drove to my appointment, my phone stopped working. Sigh. I had hoped to not have to tell my husband that I dropped it in the bathtub a couple weeks ago. But now, he's going to inspect it, and he's going to notice the grain of rice that got stuck inside it that night. (A drenched cell phone can, indeed, be restored by setting it in a bag of rice. At least, it was restored for two weeks.)

I made it to my appointment on time, and spoke pleasantly to those professional people who look at me like I am an alien. (To be fair, in that world I probably am an alien. Many people with my hormonal condition have infertility problems. Not many have six children.) My (ahem) "alternative lifestyle" is baffling and even offensive to some people. And their bewilderment is sometimes baffling and offensive to me.

As I got home from the appointment, with my non-working, rice-rattling cell phone, I noticed a coffee stain on my shirt. Had that been there for the appointment, too? Sigh. Who am I kidding? I don't belong out there! I am not one of you, you professional people of the world! You go back to reading thick books and saving lives. I'll go back to sorting through the summer clothes.

Wouldn't it be nice, indeed, if I could comfort myself by mentally congratulating myself on my own superiority to "all that?" Wouldn't it be nice if I could believe that, in God's eyes, what I do on a daily basis is more important, more beneficial to the church and the world, than what those nice-looking people do?

Wouldn't it be nice (for the frumpy, stay-at-home mom) if coffee-stained shirts and ponytails really were objectively more God-pleasing than high heels and Ph.Ds?

I know what I do is important, and I know it matters, especially to the six dear lives that matter most to me. But today I notice another weakness in myself: I notice how easy it is to forget all that, to become discontent with doing what is in front of me, and how easy it is to think I'd rather be doing what is in front of someone else. And I notice how natural it is to try to soothe that discontentment by imagining that my vocation is mysteriously way more important than everyone else's—so important, in fact, that I simply do not have time to fix my hair.

"Love one another," we are told, and "use your gifts to serve the people around you." My imperfect attempt at this looks nothing like anyone else's imperfect attempt. Why does this surprise me? God never told His children that they all should be doing the same thing. My daily bread tastes different, my daily grace is a different color.

Father, who am I to judge someone else's servant? Forgive me for looking to the left and right of me: I have not the wisdom to judge nor the right to covet. As I return from the complicated outside world into my chaotic home, equip me again to do what is in front of me. Thank you for daily bread that tastes like coffee, and the sweet breeze of fall, and the laughter of children. Pour out exactly the grace and help we need in this house to love each other and do what is in front of us. In the name of Jesus, Amen.

For further reflection

1. Do you ever wish you could live someone else's life? What type of life do you find yourself envying most often?

2. Do you ever judge others because their lives do not look like yours?

3. Read Romans 14:4:

Who are you to pass judgment on the servant of another? It is before his own master that he stands or falls. And he will be upheld, for the Lord is able to make him stand.

How does this apply to the way we see other people?

4. Is God pleased with coffee-stained mothers? Is he pleased with fancy doctors?

Explain your answer.

5. Read Romans 3:22b-24:

For there is no distinction: for all have sinned and fall short of the glory of God, and are justified by his grace as a gift, through the redemption that is in Christ Jesus.

What makes God pleased with us?

Missing the Obvious

It happens almost every Sunday morning. The kids get up and we start the day in a rush. I guzzle my coffee as we work through the list: food, clothes, teeth, hair, socks, left shoe, right shoe—all of this times six—church bags, diaper bag, bottle, sippy cup, blanket, stroller, offering. Forget the beds this morning, kids, and we will take care of the dog later. Out the door! It is time for church!

I walk with my fed and dressed kids, pushing the double stroller, smiling to myself as I imagine us as a family of ducks waddling down the road.

Then suddenly, the moment. I smile at the first friendly church-goer I see. I suddenly realize we are out in public, and I panic. *Oh no! Please tell me I remembered to change out of my pajamas!* I find to my surprise that I actually did remember; I simply forgot that I remembered.

It was one of those Sundays, when we made it to the pew and I was mentally congratulating myself on another successful Sunday morning marathon completed, with all children in their places, and not one missing his pants.

My crew and I lined up in front of the church for communion. I placed the most wiggly child directly in front of me, folded his hands, and folded mine on top of his. That is when I saw...blue fingers—mine, not his. Bright blue fingers stained with yesterday's Kool-Aid. *Oh, great! Here's another* piece of evidence for the world to see that I do not really have it all together; another obvious thing on my list that I have completely overlooked.

I reached out my blue hand to receive, and couldn't help but notice the hands that gave me Jesus: they also were stained. Not Kool-Aid, but earth stained the elder's fingers. And there was my God: held by cracked and callused fingers, and placed gently in my hands. Body and Blood, given for me, humbled to die on a cross, humbled to be held by fingers stained with work and sin.

Here in this world, where our lists are unfinished, my Lord comes. Here in my hands, these hands that find a hundred other things to do rather than fold in prayer, hands that feed children and over-feed myself, here into these hands He comes. Here, on this heart stained with vanity and distracted with the world's temptations, right here, He pours out His blood and takes away my sins.

I remember my Lord. I do not merely remember, but I taste and see Him once more. He is gracious, and He is good. My blue fingers fold in prayer and I receive the blessing.

"*May this true body and blood of our Lord Jesus Christ strengthen and preserve you in the true faith to life everlasting. Depart in peace.*"

Yes, thank you, I think I will. *Amen.*

For further reflection

1. Do you work hard to show the world that you "have it all together?"

2. Do you get upset or embarrassed when people see your mistakes or problems?

3. In Matthew 1:23, we hear an important name for Jesus:

> *"Behold, the virgin shall conceive and bear a son,*
> *and they shall call his name Immanuel"*
> *(which means, God with us).*

Is God still with us? In what ways? How do we know?

Use the following Scriptures to help you answer these questions.

> *So shall my word be that goes out from my mouth;*
> *it shall not return to me empty,*
> *but it shall accomplish that which I purpose,*
> *and shall succeed in the thing for which I sent it.*
> *(Isaiah 55:11)*

> *And I will ask the Father, and he will give you another Helper to be with you forever, even the Spirit of truth, whom the world cannot receive, because it neither sees him nor knows him. You know him, for he dwells with you and will be in you. "I will not leave you as orphans; I will come to you.*
> *(John 14:16-18)*

> *O righteous Father, even though the world does not know you, I know you, and these know that you have sent me. I made known to them your name, and I will continue to make it known, that the love with which you have loved me may be in them, and I in them."*
> *(John 17:25-26)*

Now as they were eating, Jesus took bread, and after blessing it broke it and gave it to the disciples, and said, "Take, eat; this is my body." And he took a cup, and when he had given thanks he gave it to them, saying, "Drink of it, all of you, for this is my blood of the covenant, which is poured out for many for the forgiveness of sins.
(Matthew 26:26-28)

Tangled

Every year those Christmas lights were tangled. Every single year, when the boxes came out, the complaints started. "How did these get so tangled? This is going to take all day!" I remember sitting on the carpet with lights piled in my lap, tackling the mess with impatient little fingers. If my mother dared offer help to her frustrated little girl, I would refuse and storm into another room with my project, determined to untangle at least one strand all by myself.

As an adult, I still hide away when there is untangling to be done. I have learned to accept help with Christmas lights, but when it comes to the tangled mess of my own heart, I often revert to childish methods. I wrestle in frustration. Offers of help scare me away, and I take my mess into a secret place where I can dwell on it in peace. I set my problems on my lap and try to sort out everything. I know I need to go to God for help, but I do not want to go to Him unless I can get my thoughts organized first. I imagine myself untangling things, lining them up, and sorting them into piles.

Let's see... I'll put the sins in this pile, the hormonal glitches over here, the good works over there, the medical problems here, the fears over there, the understandable weaknesses here, and the legitimate complaints I have against other people right there.

Good. Now, I have a nice, organized list of things to bring with me to God. Now, I can tell Him exactly what solution I need for each of my problems.

Of course, it never works out that way. As I wrestle, I feel more like the child who is trying so hard to untangle the Christmas lights. I pull and tug and make every effort, but I never find the beginning or the end. I work unceasingly, but my efforts only make things worse. It is still a tangled mess. The pile changes shape, but the knots are still there.

I do not bring an orderly list of concerns and requests before God. Instead, I take the tangled mess and throw it at Him in frustration. I demand that He sort it out, that He makes it right. It lies at His feet, I sulk on the floor, and I wait.

He bends down low and embraces His tangled daughter. The white robe He wears envelops us both, and it swallows up all of my tangles. For a moment, I quit fighting, and I rest in the presence of Jesus.

Father, only You can sort out the messes inside me. Cover my messes, and take my tangled self under your wing. In the name of Jesus, Amen.

For further reflection

1. Describe a time when your own heart was tangled and messy.

2. Did you ask for help? Did you hide? Were you able to sort it all out?

3. Read Romans 8:26-27:

Likewise the Spirit helps us in our weakness. For we do not know what to pray for as we ought, but the Spirit himself intercedes for us with groanings too deep for words. And he who searches hearts knows what is the mind of the Spirit, because the Spirit intercedes for the saints according to the will of God.

What does this teach you about prayer?

4. Read Isaiah 61:10:

*I will greatly rejoice in the Lord;
my soul shall exult in my God,
for he has clothed me with the garments of salvation;
he has covered me with the robe of righteousness,
as a bridegroom decks himself like a priest with a beautiful headdress,
and as a bride adorns herself with her jewels.*

Do you think this applies to you, even in your mess?

5. How do you know? Why does God save us?

*But when the goodness and loving kindness of God our Savior appeared, he saved us, not because of works done by us in righteousness, but according to his own mercy, by the washing of regeneration and renewal of the Holy Spirit, whom he poured out on us richly through Jesus Christ our Savior, so that being justified by his grace we might become heirs according to the hope of eternal life.
(Titus 3:4-7)*

But now the righteousness of God has been manifested apart from the law, although the Law and the Prophets bear witness to it— the righteousness of God through faith in Jesus

Christ for all who believe. For there is no distinction: for all have sinned and fall short of the glory of God, and are justified by his grace as a gift, through the redemption that is in Christ Jesus.
(Romans 3:21-24)

Bruises

If you are going to spend your day wrestling sinners, you are going to get bruises. This is true even if they are sinners of tiny stature. You will need bandages and crutches. You will need to ask for forgiveness and strength. You will need food for body and soul. And you probably will limp across the finish line at the end of the day.

The fourth commandment says, "You shall honor your father and mother." And when our children do not, it is sin. Yes, sin. It is not childish ignorance, but selfish, ugly sin. And sin leaves a mark.

To be fair, I leave marks, too, and daily. I am not without sin, and sin always hurts the sinner and those around the sinner. But today, I am looking at this from another angle.

Today, I remember that I am often dealing with sin in my little ones. And, though I would rather be immune to sin's effects, I bear the marks of their sin, along with my own. My heart is not made of iron, and I do not get to wear armor to work. Sin stresses me out. Sin adds darkness and ugliness to our days. Sin poisons the air.

And sin does not simply need behavior modification techniques. Sin requires repentance and forgiveness. Sinners need a Savior.

And, so, it is to Jesus I must go, both for the forgiveness of my own sin, and for the healing of the wounds I receive from the sins of others. For all of us, I pray.

> Lord, have mercy. Have mercy on me, a sinner. Lord, have mercy on my children, for they are sinners, too. In the name of Jesus, Amen.

For further reflection

1. Is there a difference between childish behavior and sin? Do you see both in your own children?

2. The fourth commandment is found in Exodus 20:12: *Honor your father and your mother, that your days may be long in the land that the LORD your God is giving you.*

Have you ever been wounded by your child because he disobeyed this commandment?

3. Describe a time when your child's sin affected your attitude in a negative way.

4. What do you think you should do when this happens?

5. "Honor your father and mother:" What does this mean in the life of a child? How does this commandment apply to you as a mother? As a daughter?

6. Read the following parable:

He also told this parable to some who trusted in themselves that they were righteous, and treated others with contempt:

"Two men went up into the temple to pray, one a Pharisee and the other a tax collector. The Pharisee, standing by himself, prayed thus: 'God, I thank you that I am not like other men, extortioners, unjust, adulterers, or even like this tax collector. I fast twice a week; I give tithes of all that I get.' But the tax collector, standing far off, would not even lift up his eyes to heaven, but beat his breast, saying, 'God, be merciful to me, a sinner!' I tell you, this man went down to his house justified, rather than the other. For everyone who exalts himself will be humbled, but the one who humbles himself will be exalted."
(Luke 18:9-14)

How does Jesus respond to the prayer, "Lord, have mercy?"

Scowling

"Mommy, look at this beautiful picture I made! I am going to bring it to school tomorrow to show my teacher!" my daughter yells. She digs through her church bag to find the picture, still breathing hard from beating all her siblings in the run home from church.

"Oh, Honey," I sigh, remembering her upcoming MRI. "It's beautiful, but you are going to have to wait until Wednesday to give it to your teacher. You don't get to go to school tomorrow; you have to go to the hospital so they can take pictures of your brain instead." "But, Mommy!" she whines, "I want to go to school!" I watch as a hard scowl squeezes the joy out of her face. She stomps down the hall, a picture of woe, certain her life is entirely ruined. I suppress a smile as I watch her moan and complain about this small misery. She doesn't even remember her year of daily seizures.

Today, it is day 445 of seizure-freedom for that girl. She has no idea what a small thing one little MRI really is.

Yet, I see myself in her, so I withhold my lecture for once. Telling her, "you think this is bad? Let me tell you how much worse it could be!" would be as unhelpful to her as it is to me when I am feeling overwhelmed and burdened. Of course, I act like her sometimes; surrounded by a million mercies, yet pitching fits over minor inconveniences. Fighting children, interrupted schedules, stomach flu, broken dishes—any one of these things has the potential to elicit sighing and complaining from me. My daughter is blessedly shielded from how much worse it really could be; and so, an MRI counts as a trial in her world. That does not make her suffering pointless, or something that can be lectured away. "God says to rejoice always, little girl, so buck up and get yourself happy, right now!"

The concept "It could be worse!" is often used by well-meaning people as an attempt to comfort those in trial. When this idea comes from a Christian, the implicit message sounds an awful lot like: "Jesus died for you! How dare you be sad?" Is this what the Bible says about suffering? Your laundry machine is broken. Rejoice always! You miss a birthday party to spend the day vomiting into a bucket. Rejoice! That baby you prayed for has died. Again I say rejoice! Really?

Christ died for us, and received the enormous suffering we deserve for our sins. Our greatest debt has been paid, and on top of that, our Heavenly Father surrounds us with His grace and blessing as His children. Surely this is reason for great joy! However, that does not mean suffering is no more. While we remain in this fallen world, we will suffer. We have not been told to wear plastic smiles and pretend it is not so.

Rejoicing and suffering often are mentioned together in Scripture. Peter wrote to the suffering church, "*In this you greatly rejoice, though now for a little while you may have had to suffer grief in all kinds of trials*"

(1 Peter 1:6). Trials, from minor inconveniences to breath-taking grief, have been part of the life of the Christian since the beginning. The imperative "rejoice!" is not intended to be a heavy word of Law slapped on the back of a suffering Christian. It is not a call to rack our brains for a hundred reasons to be thankful even as we tremble under the shadow of death. God's children suffer, sometimes greatly, sometimes without knowing why. And yet they are made able to rejoice even while suffering.

The important question is: rejoice in what? Surely not in the fact that they suffer! No, rather read the beautiful words Peter uses to direct the eyes of His fellow saints to their source of joy:

In his great mercy he has given us new birth into a living hope through the resurrection of Jesus Christ from the dead, and into an inheritance that can never perish, spoil, or fade— kept in heaven for you, who through faith are shielded by God's power until the coming of salvation that is ready to be revealed in the last time. (1 Peter 1:3-5)

In *this* we greatly rejoice, though now, for a little while, we suffer grief in all kinds of trials. As God's children, we have been given so much more to comfort us than "It could be worse!" We have a risen Savior, a certain hope, and a God who keeps our inheritance for us, Who will carry us through our trials to that day when we are with Him in eternity. We may sigh today, we may even mourn; yet, even as we do these things, we are tenderly invited to look to that day when the promises God has given us in Christ will be fulfilled. Soon, we will be gathered with all His saints, and He will destroy for us every reason for scowling or tears.

Father,

Teach us what it means to rejoice, even in this place of suffering. Here we suffer irritations and annoyances, as well as real griefs and tragedies. In all things, be our comfort and our strength. Lift up our heads, that we may look forward to Your coming, and the end of our suffering in Your promises fulfilled. In the name of Jesus, Amen.

For further reflection

1. Are you ever tempted to minimize your children's suffering, as the author was? What might you do instead?

2. Read 2 Corinthians 1:5-7:

For as we share abundantly in Christ's sufferings, so through Christ we share abundantly in comfort, too. If we are afflicted, it is for your comfort and salvation; and if we are comforted, it is for your comfort, which you experience when you patiently endure the same sufferings that we suffer. Our hope for you is unshaken, for we know that as you share in our sufferings, you will also share in our comfort.

What do we all share in as Christians?

3. What has happened in your life recently that has led you to complaining?

4. Do you think it is OK for us to bring our complaints to God?

5. Read Psalm 22:1-11:

> *My God, my God, why have you forsaken me?*
> *Why are you so far from saving me, from the words of my groaning?*
> *O my God, I cry by day, but you do not answer, and by night, but I find no rest.*
> *Yet you are holy, enthroned on the praises of Israel.*
> *In you our fathers trusted; they trusted, and you delivered them.*
> *To you they cried and were rescued; in you they trusted and were not put to shame.*
> *But I am a worm and not a man, scorned by mankind and despised by the people.*
> *All who see me mock me; they make mouths at me; they wag their heads;*
> *"He trusts in the Lord; let him deliver him; let him rescue him, for he delights in him!"*
> *Yet you are he who took me from the womb; you made me trust you at my mother's breasts.*
> *On you was I cast from my birth, and from my mother's womb you have been my God.*
> *Be not far from me, for trouble is near, and there is none to help.*

Does that sound like a complaint? How is this different from simply whining?

6. Since we are to expect suffering in this world, how can there still be joy? Read the following verses for help:

> Therefore, since we have been justified by faith, we have peace with God through our Lord Jesus Christ. Through him we have also obtained access by faith into this grace in which we stand, and we rejoice in hope of the glory of God. Not only that, but we rejoice in our sufferings, knowing that suffering produces endurance, and endurance produces character, and character produces hope, and hope does not put us to shame, because God's love has been poured into our hearts through the Holy Spirit who has been given to us. For while we were still weak, at the right time Christ died for the ungodly. For one will scarcely die for a righteous person—though perhaps for a good person one would dare even to die—but God shows his love for us in that while we were still sinners, Christ died for us. Since, therefore, we have now been justified by his blood, much more shall we be saved by him from the wrath of God. For if while we were enemies we were reconciled to God by the death of his Son, much more, now that we are reconciled, shall we be saved by his life. More than that, we also rejoice in God through our Lord Jesus Christ, through whom we have now received reconciliation.
> (Romans 5:1-11)

Kicking It In

When I ran track in high-school, middle-distance was my "specialty." This was not my choice, but it was my lot. I was not built to sprint, and I was too wimpy to train harder for long distance. So by default, the half-mile became my race.

I was in extremely good shape at that time, and I remember running at nearly full speed for that entire half mile. I remember the muscle fatigue, the absolute exhaustion and burning lungs that seemed to persist through the whole race. I remember getting a little dizzy and feeling the temptation to slow down. I remember the rock that marked the spot where I was told to "kick it in," the last 150 yards of the race where I was supposed to draw on strength from who knows where and go even faster when what I really wanted to do was lie down on the soft grass.

The rock meant "it's almost over!" and so was a welcomed sight. Yet it also meant one last burst of energy, muscle pain everywhere, and becoming so tired my eyes no longer wanted to focus. The final efforts squeezed the absolute last drops of energy out of me, until finally, the finish line, the collapse, and the eventual catching of breath.

What made me think of this experience this week? My evenings, that last stretch, between about 6:30 p.m. and 8:30 p.m. The end of dinner has become my new "rock," the marker that reminds me, "you're almost there!" It encourages me to pour out the last drops of energy for the last 100—minutes, that is—until I can collapse.

My list after dinner: kitchen cleaned, coffee ready for tomorrow, baths perhaps, 6 children in PJs, three in diapers, teeth brushed, clothes out for tomorrow, lunches packed, homework checked, buddies located, music on, closet doors closed, night lights on, "hug kiss and tucks," breaking up the last few fights, and then finally, quiet.

By the close of dinner, I am out of words, or at least I would like to be. I have kept pace with the kid chatter all day long and I just feel like there are no words left inside me at all. Yet, as I go through my list, their words continue to bombard me.

"Mommy, we forgot to do my word cards! Can you do them with me?"

"He dumped water on the floor, Mommy!"

"Mommy, where is my Curious George?"

"Mommy, Daddy's reading to him. Can you read to me?"

"Can we wrestle?"

"Mommy! He's watching me put my PJs on! MAKE HIM STOP!"

"Can we go to the park?" (No, it's dark out.)

"Can we go tomorrow?"

"Someone didn't flush the potty!"

"Can we watch a movie?" (No.)

"OK, then, can we tomorrow?"

"I can't open the toothpaste!"

"Can we paint?" (No.)

"OK, then, can we tomorrow? When can we?"

"Mommy, when can we go to Michigan again?"

"Mommy, look at this beautiful picture! Can we send it to grandma right now?"

"Mommy, can we listen to the story about the flower girl?"

"Mommy, can you brush my hair? Button my PJs? Find my blanket? Kiss me, tuck me, tickle me?"

Inside I say to myself, "You can do it, just a little bit more, you're almost there, just a couple more things, and the house will be quiet soon... kick it in, kick it in, kick it in!"

But it's not like track. Yes, I am exhausted. Yes, it would be more efficient and I would get to collapse sooner if I rushed through the last part of the night as quickly as possible. But, the race is no longer about simply getting a good time. It's about finishing the race with kindness, with grace. It's time to tuck them in and share their giggles, and say "I love you" in a way that actually communicates "I love you" and not "Oh, please, just stop talking now." For me, this is about as natural as running with grace, or even worse, cheer-leading.

God, give me strength for that last hour of the day! Give strength to my muscles and to my heart, and teach me to finish the race of the day with grace! I need to borrow all of it from You! Amen.

For further reflection

1. As a mother, what time of day is hardest for you?

2. Do you have a bedtime routine that includes prayer and God's Word? If not, consider starting a simple ritual with your child. It is never too early to feed your baby the Word of Life.

3. Do you ever rush through bedtime and wish you hadn't?

4. Read Deuteronomy 11: 18-19:

You shall therefore lay up these words of mine in your heart and in your soul, and you shall bind them as a sign on your hand, and they shall be as frontlets between your eyes. You shall teach them to your children, talking of them when you are sitting in your house, and when you are walking by the way, and when you lie down, and when you rise.

In what way does God want His Word to be part of your home life?

5. Read Galatians 5:22-23:

But the fruit of the Spirit is love, joy, peace, patience, kindness, goodness, faithfulness, gentleness, self-control.

Where do love, patience, gentleness, and all these good things come from?

6. Consider how you might use what you just learned to help you through the hardest part of your day.

Tending

"I'll finish our book in a minute, Honey. I need to tend to the baby."

I use the verb "tend " all the time to refer to the baby of the house. I hear crying or fussing, and I rush off to "tend," to meet whatever need it is that needs meeting. I tell the other children I must "tend," because as I go to pick up the baby I do not know whether he needs changing or feeding or cuddling or whatever. Wait a minute, big kids, Mommy needs to "tend!"

I remember when baby number five was little and needed tending to, and my daughter was sick and needed so much tending to, and the others tended to each other as much as possible. I remember the day I was cooking dinner and talking to baby and dosing up the epilepsy medicine, when one of the big kids pulled on my leg and demanded with big sad eyes, "Mommy! Tend to *me*!"

I like the verb "tend," and I have begun to use it in my prayers. I use it when I pray for my family that is close to my heart but far from my house, doing things during their days that I know nothing about. I pray that God tends to them in their day-to-day struggles. There are some in our church family who suffer, and I don't know what to pray or how to help them. So I use that wonderful verb that covers it all: I pray that Jesus tends to them. He knows whatever needs there are that must be met, and He is able to meet them.

Jesus, please tend to those I love near and far. Tend to those who are rejoicing for I know not what, for those who bear sadness and trials that I do not see. Tend to those who miss loved ones, tend to those who suffer, tend to those who need you. Jesus, our Good Shepherd, tend to us. Amen.

For further reflection

1. Is there someone on your heart that you want to pray for, but you don't know how?

2. Read Hebrews 7:25:

Consequently, he is able to save to the uttermost those who draw near to God through him, since he always lives to make intercession for them.

What does Jesus live to do?

3. Read Romans 8:31-39:

What then shall we say to these things? If God is for us, who can be against us? He who did not spare his own Son but gave him up for us all, how will he not also with him graciously give us all things? Who shall bring any charge against God's elect? It is God who justifies. Who is to condemn? Christ Jesus is the one who died—more than that, who was raised—who is at the right hand of God, who indeed is interceding for us. Who shall separate us from the love of Christ? Shall tribulation, or distress, or persecution, or famine, or nakedness, or danger, or sword? As it is written,

> *"For your sake we are being killed all the day long;*
> *we are regarded as sheep to be slaughtered."*
> *No, in all these things we are more than conquerors through him who loved us. For I am sure that neither death nor life, nor angels nor rulers, nor things present nor things to come, nor powers, nor height nor depth, nor anything else in all creation, will be able to separate us from the love of God in Christ Jesus our Lord.*

Again, what does Jesus do for us? What in this passage gives you comfort, both for you and for those on your heart?

4. Read Psalm 23:

> *The Lord is my shepherd; I shall not want.*
> *He makes me lie down in green pastures.*
> *He leads me beside still waters.*
> *He restores my soul.*
> *He leads me in paths of righteousness*
> *for his name's sake.*
> *Even though I walk through the valley of the shadow of death,*
> *I will fear no evil,*
> *for you are with me;*
> *your rod and your staff,*
> *they comfort me.*
> *You prepare a table before me*
> *in the presence of my enemies;*
> *you anoint my head with oil;*
> *my cup overflows.*
> *Surely goodness and mercy shall follow me*
> *all the days of my life,*
> *and I shall dwell in the house of the Lord*
> *forever.*

What does this teach you about how God cares for His children?

Use this passage as a basis for your prayers for those you know who are suffering.

What Do You Have That You Did Not Receive?

The baby screamed for an hour for Daddy. When I returned, we sat together, he nursed, and then he closed his eyes in happy contentment. What an amazing blessing it is to have exactly, completely, what my dear child needs in this moment.

What do I have, what do I give to him that I did not receive? Did I invent this perfect system of baby-soothing? Did I fret and research and stock up on the things I thought my son might need? Did I, through effort, make my body to be the soft, flabby pillow that my child needs at this moment? Of course not. God knew what he needed and gave it all to me, and I get to give it to him.

But these babies of mine, they grow. And big kids are not so easy to satisfy. They are learning more reasons for crying and fear, and all cannot be soothed by the softness of a mother's embrace.

I fret about the days to come. I fret because I have to give room for the spreading of wings in a terrifying world. I fret because the problems they face grow as their years increase. I fret because I consider my own resources, and they are woefully lacking. I fret because I will have to share. I must trust God to meet their needs... and accept that He often will do that without my help.

Yet, He who has promised will be faithful, not only to them but also to me.

What do I have that I did not receive? And what I have lacked so far?

Heavenly Father, You have been faithful to me. I have received from Your hand all that I have needed so far to care for these dear children. Yet I worry, Father, as I consider the years to come. I see my sin and my lack, but You are and will be faithful to provide. You see me: I am needed, I am needy. You have given, and You will give again and again according to Your Word, according to Your great mercy that You have shown me in Jesus. Lead me on, Lord, and fill my open hands with daily bread. Amen.

For further reflection

1. What have you received from God that you pass on to your children? List several things.

2. Are your children starting to need you less? How do you feel about that?

3. Read Jeremiah 29:11:

For I know the plans I have for you, declares the Lord, plans for welfare and not for evil, to give you a future and a hope.

Consider how this applies to both you and your children.

4. Read Proverbs 3:5-6:

> *Trust in the Lord with all your heart,*
> *and do not lean on your own understanding.*
> *In all your ways acknowledge him,*
> *and he will make straight your paths.*

What does God invite you to do? Who is directing your paths?

6. Now consider your children. Are they learning to trust in God and to look to Him to direct their paths?

Held in Peace

"And the peace of God, which passes all understanding, will guard and keep your hearts and minds in Christ Jesus." (Philippians 4:7)

Doesn't it seem strange to talk about "peace" in this place where tornadoes destroy and babies die? What is this peace that we have in Christ? Does the peace of God somehow lift us above the fear and grief that is part of the human condition?

Christians suffer, in body and in spirit in this place. We are not given the peace of the stoic. We are not told to smile when all is well, and smile when the cancer is terminal. We are not told to close our hearts to that which could disturb our peace. We do not experience a mystical inner connection with God that allows us to weather the storms of this life like immovable statues. No, we flip and fly with the winds, much like the rest of the world. In our experience, we who have peace with Christ often do not feel very peaceful at all, not in this place. Christians suffer, and yet there *is* peace in Christ.

Those who are not in Christ are like a kite, unfettered, free-wheeling through the sky, vulnerable to the winds and the elements. The crash is inevitable. The flight is terrifying.

We who have Christ are like the kite held by the strong father. We still are assaulted by the winds.

The rain falls, and some of the turns make our stomachs lurch. We may even feel as if we are careening out of control, and we brace for impact. But even in the worst of storms, we are tethered to a Rock. We are held fast by Him who loves us.

As we flip and fly in this life, we know that nothing that assaults us can force us out of his hands. He will hold us fast. And one day He will reel us in, to Himself. He will bring us to our home of forever peace, in perfect safety. Until then, even as we flip and fly, His grip is our peace.

Heavenly Father, Hold me tight, in the calm and in the storm. Wrap me in Your love for me, and give me peace. In the name of Jesus, Amen.

For further reflection

1. Do you struggle with anxiety? What sorts of things make you anxious?

2. Read Hebrews 12:1-2:

> *Therefore, since we are surrounded by so great a cloud of witnesses, let us also lay aside every weight, and sin which clings so closely, and let us run with endurance the race that is set before us, looking to Jesus, the founder and perfecter of our faith, who for the joy that was set before him endured the cross, despising the shame, and is seated at the right hand of the throne of God.*

Where should we be looking? What do we learn about Him from this passage?

3. Read Psalm 27:1-5:

> The Lord is my light and my salvation;
> whom shall I fear?
> The Lord is the stronghold of my life;
> of whom shall I be afraid?
> When evildoers assail me
> to eat up my flesh,
> my adversaries and foes,
> it is they who stumble and fall.
> Though an army encamp against me,
> my heart shall not fear;
> though war arise against me,
> yet I will be confident.
> One thing have I asked of the Lord,
> that will I seek after:
> that I may dwell in the house of the Lord
> all the days of my life,
> to gaze upon the beauty of the Lord
> and to inquire in his temple.
> For he will hide me in his shelter
> in the day of trouble;
> he will conceal me under the cover of his tent;
> he will lift me high upon a rock.

Where is David's heart fixed? What does He want from God? What will God do for him (and for you) in the day of trouble?

4. Read Philippians 4:4-8:

Rejoice in the Lord always; again I will say, rejoice. Let your reasonableness be known to everyone. The Lord is at hand; do not be anxious about anything, but in everything by prayer and supplication with thanksgiving let your requests be made known to God. And the peace of God, which surpasses all understanding, will guard your hearts and your minds in Christ Jesus.
Finally, brothers, whatever is true, whatever is honorable, whatever is just, whatever is pure, whatever is lovely, whatever is commendable, if there is any excellence, if there is anything worthy of praise, think about these things.

Pray to the God of peace, that He would give you a peaceful mind and heart, fixed on Him and on whatever is good. Use this Scripture for guidance in your prayers.

Tired Explorer

There are few things as disruptive as the cantankerousness of a teething baby.

There are few sounds so pleasantly received as the tiny snores of said baby after he has been wrestled to sleep.

With my little explorer in my tired arms, I lingered in the rocking chair long after he finally melted into them. Too tired to be hurried, I smiled at the spiky flip of his hair, the last bit of evidence of his angry mood that had finally been soothed away. Soft arms, Tylenol, and a few pats on the back had vanquished the evil foe. A forgotten tear rested in the corner of his eye. I used my smallest finger to wipe away the tiny sadness.

This is but the beginning of pains, Dear One. Easily I soothe your physical pain, but what of the heart-suffering that this world will bring? Oh, son, our peace in this rocking chair is so brittle.

His journey has started sweetly, but how far must he travel? Through what dark and awful valleys? Which arrows of suffering will pierce his precious body and soul along the way?

Mere rocking soothed him to sleep, but what of my growing pains, Lord? Are these beginnings? Is it noontime? Or might this old sun be setting soon? I try to imagine life after the dying sun sets and the eternal sun rises: A real finish line for trials; a sweet beginning of untainted eternal joys; peace unbreakable; pain silenced; fear destroyed; life abundant; life everlasting.

These concepts are so foreign to my experience that they sound like fantasy. Yet, a foretaste of peace in a rocking chair, a tincture of grace from a chalice — these things make my heart and soul long for the day when God's work is completed. I will be the tired explorer, and He will welcome me into His arms. And then, finally, He will wipe away the last drop of heart-suffering from the corner of my eye.

Father, Thank you for the foretaste of peace you give in the rocking chair, and in Your Word and Sacraments. Sustain my faith, and the faith of my little ones, until that day when You call us home. In the name of Jesus, Amen.

For further reflection

1. Will you suffer as a Christian in this life? What insights do you gain from the following verses?

> *Truly, truly, I say to you, you will weep and lament, but the world will rejoice. You will be sorrowful, but your sorrow will turn into joy. When a woman is giving birth, she has sorrow because her hour has come, but when she has delivered the baby, she no longer remembers the anguish, for joy that a human being has been born into the world. So also you have sorrow now, but I will see you again, and your hearts will rejoice, and no one will take your joy from you.*
> *(John 16:20-22)*

> *Beloved, do not be surprised at the fiery trial when it comes upon you to test you, as though something strange were happening to you.*
> *(1 Peter 4:12)*
>
> *You, however, have followed my teaching, my conduct, my aim in life, my faith, my patience, my love, my steadfastness, my persecutions and sufferings that happened to me at Antioch, at Iconium, and at Lystra—which persecutions I endured; yet from them all the Lord rescued me. Indeed, all who desire to live a godly life in Christ Jesus will be persecuted, while evil people and impostors will go on from bad to worse, deceiving and being deceived.*
> *(2 Timothy 3:10-13)*

2. Will your children also suffer?

3. Read 2 Timothy 3:14-17:

> *But as for you, continue in what you have learned and have firmly believed, knowing from whom you learned it and how from childhood you have been acquainted with the sacred writings, which are able to make you wise for salvation through faith in Christ Jesus. All Scripture is breathed out by God and profitable for teaching, for reproof, for correction, and for training in righteousness, that the man of God may be complete, equipped for every good work.*

How can you and your children be prepared for the suffering you will face in this world?

4. Read John 16:33:

> *[Jesus said,] I have said these things to you, that in me you may have peace. In the world you will have tribulation. But take heart; I have overcome the world.*

What comfort do we have as God's children, even when everything in this world is falling apart?

5. Read Revelation 21:1-7:

> Then I saw a new heaven and a new earth, for the first heaven and the first earth had passed away, and the sea was no more. And I saw the holy city, new Jerusalem, coming down out of heaven from God, prepared as a bride adorned for her husband. And I heard a loud voice from the throne saying, "Behold, the dwelling place of God is with man. He will dwell with them, and they will be his people, and God himself will be with them as their God. He will wipe away every tear from their eyes, and death shall be no more, neither shall there be mourning, nor crying, nor pain anymore, for the former things have passed away."
> And he who was seated on the throne said, "Behold, I am making all things new." Also he said, "Write this down, for these words are trustworthy and true." And he said to me, "It is done! I am the Alpha and the Omega, the beginning and the end. To the thirsty I will give from the spring of the water of life without payment. The one who conquers will have this heritage, and I will be his God and he will be my son.

Imagine what it will be like for you and your children on that day. Write your thoughts and prayers here.

Conclusion

An excerpt from <u>Weak and Loved: A Mother-Daughter Love Story</u>
by Emily Cook

To Aggie, my nap buddy

Aggie Sue, I love when you are my nap buddy. To see my little tornado still and calm is a rare treat. I love the way you ask to hold my hand until you fall asleep.

Today you had a long seizure right before nap time that made you so tired you were asleep in my bed even before I laid down the other kids. I climbed in next to you anyway. I just wanted to be close to you. I held your little hand.

Like so many times before, I rested next to you and stroked your hair. My heart loved and ached, and my eyes were relieved to release a few tears that had been sitting there all day. As I sighed over your raccoon eyes and stroked your hair, I wondered where on that beautiful head they would cut should they have to do surgery. My spirit prayed fervently to the God who loves us both.

We laid there in the sunshine, and you snored peacefully as I wrestled with my worries. The sun shone brightly even through the blinds, and soon I found myself relaxing into the quiet and warmth of the bed.

I thank God for that moment, when you and I lay there in the sun, wrapped in warm blankets and love, enjoying a green pasture before our journey through the valley.

We have darkness to go through yet, my dear child. I am sure we often will hold hands through the darkness as we are doing now. I suspect we will be separated for some of it. I know we will be carried through all of it by Him who loves us both, the One who has been there before. But for this sweet moment, we rest on our pillows that smell like home.

I wonder, after the days of valleys and darkness, will we be given moments like this again? Will we rest together, hold hands, and enjoy the warmth of each others' love on pillows that smell like Home? Will we give goodnight kisses, smile, say I love you for the millionth time, in that Other place? Perhaps then the shadows of this valley will be distant memories. Perhaps the sun will be the Light of Christ, the light that chased away our fears and pain, and our "I love yous" will finally be sweet and pure and simple.

<u>Weak and Loved: A Mother-Daughter Love Story</u> is now available for purchase on Amazon.com

"…when she was often reduced to nothing, God carried her through, with or without her cooperation, her understanding or acceptance. This book helped me understand what true grace really is – the totally undeserved, bountiful love of God, which no circumstances can ever take away from us." – bookie, on Amazon.com

ISBN-13 (978-1466484313)
ISBN-10 (1466484314)

*If you enjoyed this book,
please share it with a friend.*

*Permission granted to reproduce all or part of
this publication with due credit given to the author.*

*Visit www.weakandloved.com
for more by Emily Cook.*

Project 24

All profits from sales of *Tend to Me* will be donated to Project 24.

Project 24 is a service project dedicated to building at least 24 orphan rescue centers throughout Kenya. Financial donations are collected from caring people around the world and used to construct safe homes, as well as provide food, clothing, and healthcare for children in need. As their physical needs are met, each child is also told of the love of Jesus.

For more information, visit
http://www.weakandloved.com/p/project-24.html

Made in the USA
San Bernardino, CA
16 January 2017